One of the most thought-provoking books [illegible] ever read. I urge all readers, from all paths, to read it carefully and to slowly digest the writer's message. I offer this with a warning: do not kindly dismiss these words with the thought, 'I already know that.' Even if you do, you probably need reminding: Two thousand years of religious potty-training doesn't necessarily disappear overnight.

—Christine Hall, Editor, Alternative Approaches Magazine, Pinnacle, North Carolina

I was overwhelmed. There have been many who have abstractly mulled over these very same thoughts about the dogmas of organized religions, but the brilliance of this book is its success in driving home the message with such compelling effectiveness. It is the antidote for so many of today's problems.

—Parthiv N. Parekh, Editor, Khabar Magazine, Norcross, Georgia

This book is another Kahlil Gibran-caliber 'The Prophet.'

—Astrid Ware, Author, Los Angeles, California

I believe the words of this unique book, like the words of timeless peacemakers, such as Mahatma Gandhi, Thich Nhat Hanh and Kahlil Gibran, will prevail to the benefit of all who read it, and should occupy a place on the shelf of every caring human being.

—Tim O'Hagan, Cape Town, South Africa; author/editor of 11 books, including Discovering the Wonders of Our World, by Reader's Digest; the Reader's Digest Guide to Alternative Medicine, and Spectacular World of Southern African Wildlife (Reader's Digest)

WARPAINT OF THE GODS

Essential Thinking
For The
New Millennium

NILA SAGADEVAN

Foreword by Tim O'Hagan

ISBN: 0-9762606-0-3

Library of Congress Catalog Card Number 2004098448
(B – Philosophy, Psychology, Religion)
1. Self-actualization. 2. Spirituality. 3.Metaphysical

First Printing January 2005
Printed in Canada

Book design by Fiona Raven
Cover illustration by Kishan Muthucumaru

Published by Truepenny Media, Inc.
Laguna Hills, California

TRUEPENNY MEDIA

Truepenny Media, Inc.
PO Box 2177
Laguna Hills, CA
USA 92654-2177
www.TruepennyMedia.com

To the one God, the universal One

this book is humbly dedicated

Table of Contents

Foreword

BY TIM O'HAGAN

The past few centuries have witnessed the golden age of humankind. Our extraordinary species has evolved from a primeval and disparate band of Neanderthal creatures wielding Stone Age hand axes into a highly sophisticated global community which continues to astound itself with its scientific acumen and technological wizardry. We have probed the frontiers of space, mastered the art of genetic engineering, developed a microscope which can discriminate atoms, and produced a $100-million computer capable of performing 360 trillion operations per second.

But in spite of our awesome evolution, another, faster computer—the human brain—has failed to make the most important discovery of all: how to live peacefully with other human beings. While our tiny planet remains a speck of dust in the endless realms of the Universe, and our lives remain a mere tick in the clock of Cosmic time, we have chosen to use this time to murder our own kind on a scale that doesn't bear thinking. Worse still, we have chosen the very God that created universal life as the implement for waging wars of mass destruction; the *casus belli* of our killing fields.

During the 20th Century alone 110 million people were killed by their own kind in 250 wars —that's six times more people than were killed in wars the previous century. While it is impossible to assert how many have died as a result of religious conflict, history has shown that religious wars in the name of sectarian "gods" have bathed God's beautiful Earth in human blood and violated the sanctity of human life on an incomprehensible scale.

In *Warpaint of the Gods,* Nila Sagadevan makes an eloquent and impassioned plea for the universal acceptance of peace and an end to the ceaseless cycle of slaughter driven by so many religions in the name of a God. Sagadevan provides a compelling insight into the very nature of humankind and how humans have abrogated and abused the very tenets of civilization in the name of religion. More importantly, the author shows how the course of life on our planet could change irrevocably if humans made the simple paradigm shift from self-righteous ethnocentricity to common kindness, and the universal acceptance that there is one great God.

He argues, with seasoned logic and a rare objectivity, that we are not alone in the Universe; that other life in the Cosmos is not only probable but entirely reasonable, and that the time will come when this will be established as fact. I believe the words of this unique book, like the words of timeless peacemakers, such as Mahatma Gandhi, Thich Nhat Hanh and Kahlil Gibran, will prevail to the benefit of all who read it, and should occupy a place on the shelf of every caring human being.

Tim O'Hagan is the author of 11 books and has contributed to or edited more than two dozen local and global titles, including Discovering the Wonders of Our World, by Reader's Digest; the Reader's Digest Guide to Alternative Medicine; Spectacular World of Southern African Wildlife (Reader's Digest); Wild Places of Southern Africa (Struik); and Desertscapes of Namibia (Struik).

Preface

↔

I have been deeply saddened by the rampant savagery of our present age, and feel the message of this book could not come at a more appropriate or pressing time.

As I write this, countless conflicts are ravaging this planet "in the name of God." Jews and Muslims are destroying each other in the name of their gods. Catholics and Protestants are murdering each other to appease their gods. Hindus and Sikhs are annihilating each other to pacify their gods. Christians and Muslims are butchering each other for the sake of their gods. Buddhists and Hindus are brutalizing each other to pay homage to their gods...

Warpaint Of The Gods contains the pith of my personal observations and experience of this numbing insanity. In this book I try to present my convictions clearly, logically, and in a non-sectarian manner, in the hope it reaches people of all religious denominations throughout the world. I have taken special care not to trespass on individual religious beliefs or offend those who subscribe to them.

This book aims to introduce a voice of reason to the paradox of religious bloodshed which pervades the world today. It also invites the reader to stroll down fresh, possibly uncharted, paths. It certainly does not intend to proselytize, or encourage readers to abandon their religious principles or line of thinking. Therefore, should the words in the following pages offend or bruise the reader's personal beliefs in any way, I offer my apologies in advance.

No intelligent argument denying that "war is the business of barbarians" can be sustained for long. This truism embodies a certain fundamental logic that resonates with any rational intellect that would care to ponder this most heinous of human behavior.

But war waged "in the name of God" reduces our rational processes to an irrational absolute. Such a concept defies all logic and reason, as any argument supporting it can only be born of a desperately irrational posture rooted in blind faith. It is not unreasonable to deduce, then, that such a mindset is not merely primitive as a cerebral construct, but is also ultimately self-destructive.

The premise of this book is my deep, passionate belief that only non-institutional, non-dogmatic spirituality, and not organized religion, can bring peace to this planet.

Steven Weinberg, Nobel Prize winner in Physics in 1979, said during his acceptance speech: "With or without religion, you would have good people doing good things and evil people doing evil things. But for good people to do evil things, that takes religion." *Warpaint Of The Gods* essentially expands on Mr. Weinberg's profound observation.

The intent of this book is not to be a treatise, but an invocation. Ergo, its success can only be measured by the minds it awakens. Lest such an aspiration appears to be more immodest than noble, I humbly say this: If it kindles just one receptive spark in the nameless natural Luminosity that resides at the core of all God's sentient creations, in some kindred soul somewhere on this planet, I will deem this book a resounding success.

Laguna Hills, California
July 17, 2004

I'm not trying to counsel any of you to do anything really special except to dare to think and to dare to go with the truth and to dare to really love completely.

—R. BUCKMINSTER FULLER

During a recent interview on CNN,

Carlos Santana was asked,

"What is your religion?"

Santana:

"If you can tell me God's religion,

that is my religion."

Does God have a "religion"?

If He does,

What is it?

If He does not…

Why do we humans

have so many?

Can one love and worship God

with all one's heart

and soul…

…yet belong to no "religion"?

Essential Thinking

For The

New Millennium

NILA SAGADEVAN

Foreword by Tim O'Hagan

The world has achieved brilliance without wisdom, power without conscience. Ours is a world of nuclear giants and ethical infants. We know more about war than we know about peace, more about killing than we know about living.

—GENERAL OMAR BRADLEY

✧

CHAPTER I

Mindless Hatred

Time does not—*cannot*—mitigate the innate barbarity of war.

Whether motivated by thinly veiled escapism or downright denial, we never tire of trying to convince ourselves that we've risen above the ageless human predisposition for savagery. Perhaps we find it absolving, cathartic even, to look back across aeons of human conflict and see War as the odious province of our barbaric forebears. It's as if this sort of forcibly distant, almost antiseptically nostalgic

*The most persistent sound which
reverberates through men's history
is the beating of war drums.*

—Arthur Koestler

view makes it easier for us to separate our modern warmongering from its brutish past, and elevate our own behavior to a loftier, more "civilized"—and thus acceptable—plane.

But regardless of its chronological context, and no matter how one chooses to couch it, war remains chained to its invariably (and conveniently) ignored synonym: Murder.

Whether modern or medieval, war is, and will forever remain, mass murder. However hard we may try, the inherent brutality of war cannot be reformed; it cannot be absolved; it cannot be codified. However eloquently we may strive to clothe its beastly nature with the silks of intellectual rationale ("conventions"), technological sophistry ("smart bombs"), and political puffery ("liberation"), war cannot be dressed in decency. Stripped naked, it stands in all its ghoulish glory for what it is: Murder.

*It is my conviction that killing
under the cloak of war is
nothing but an act of murder.*

—ALBERT EINSTEIN

But murder *"in the name of God"* raises this mindless practice to a numbing level of insanity, one that transcends the obvious ideological paradox of the expression, and bestows upon it a uniquely demented distinction: the quintessential oxymoron.

Even in our "modern" age—that of reason, gentility, diplomacy and the rest of it—we do not see this singularly contradictory psychosis for the twisted concept that it is. Indeed, it actually *fuels* our macabre engines of prejudice, chauvinism, and hatred.

As the world continues to watch all too complacently, the bloodbaths continue, and human evolution perpetuates its history as a tragic parade of fratricidal butchery perpetrated in the name of God.

↤

Religion professes peace (and the sincerity of the professors is not being doubted), but it always turns out to have a dominant part in any war that is going or contemplated.

—HOWARD NEMEROV

As I write this, the world is awash with blood spilt in the name of God. Jews and Muslims are destroying each other in the names of their gods, although they share common prophets.

Catholics and Protestants are murdering each other to appease their gods, and both groups are essentially Christian.

Hindus and Sikhs are annihilating each other to pacify their gods, and the founder of Sikhism was a Hindu.

Christians and Muslims are butchering each other for the sake of their gods, and they have many saints in common.

Buddhists and Hindus are brutalizing each other to pay homage to their gods, and the Buddha was born a Hindu.

And it continues *ad nauseam*.

↔

*There is no…difference between
one religion and another, because
each religion embodies the ultimate
Truth…there is only one Truth,
but it is called different names
by different people…religions
will never differ when it is a
matter of the highest Truth.*

—SRI CHINMOY

This raises the question: Is there really more than one God?

↶

For instance, most Westerners believe "Allah" to be the name of some sovereign Muslim deity. In fact, Allah is simply the Arabic word for God. People are shocked to discover that Arab Christians and Jews refer to God as Allah (the media never tell us these things; that would only soften the face of the enemy and dissipate our war cries).

Could all these different religions worship the same God, despite the dogma that tells them otherwise?

Judging by the human carnage that trails into antiquity, religions are hardly the loving, uplifting panacea to mankind's moral ills they were intended to be.

Rather, they have transmuted into wrathful,

*Men never do evil so completely
and cheerfully as when they do
it from religious conviction.*

—BLAISE PASCAL

selfish albatrosses that have kept us spiritually blind, separated, and fueled with wanton internecine hatred.

Nations have been built and destroyed, civilizations raised and razed, billions butchered across centuries—all in the name of one group or another's idea of God. (It could be argued that not all wars are fought in the name of God, but those who engage in wars almost always have "God on their side." One way or the other, God is involved.)

Is it not time that we rose above the divisive dogmas of our earthly religions?

Is it not time to realize that the path to our awakening as an intelligent species requires neither the doctrinaire "guidance" nor "facilitation" dispensed by our various organized religions?

Is it not time that we were collectively

When we blindly adopt a
religion…we become automatons.
We cease to grow.

—ANAIS NIN

deprogrammed from our blind adherence to dogma and awakened to the essential reality of one loving Creator?

If not now, when?

*A religious awakening which
does not awaken the sleeper to
love has roused him in vain.*

—JESSAMYN WEST

⊷

CHAPTER 2

Growth

It is time we awoke to our innate potential for direct connection with the spiritual inheritance that dwells within every one of us.

Especially at this perilous juncture in our evolution, it is vital that we awaken—truly awaken—to the central truth that, regardless of individual religious persuasion, each of us worships the same loving Creator.

This pivotal realization would help begin the huge task of breaking down the religious walls that compartmentalize mankind and

*The intuitive mind is a sacred
gift and the rational mind is a
faithful servant. We have created
a society that honors the servant
and has forgotten the gift.*

—ALBERT EINSTEIN

opening our understanding to the innate, divinely imbued core of love within each of us.

However, while many people pay noisy lip service to this concept, our conduct on the world's stage only reveals our utter ignorance of it. The more technological advances we make, the more detached we become from the common thread of divine love that exists within all life.

True, we have mastered relatively complex technologies, even broken our earthly bonds and ventured to our moon (although, given our primitive forms of chemical propulsion, this achievement could be unimpressive to more advanced civilizations). But, even with all our impressive technologies and conveniences, nothing fundamental *within* us has changed.

Cruise missiles and directed energy weapons

*What we now want is closer
contact and better understanding
between individuals and
communities all over the earth,
and the elimination of egoism and
pride which is always prone to
plunge the world into primeval
barbarism and strife. Peace can
only come as a natural consequence
of universal enlightenment.*

—Nikola Tesla

do not make us more "evolved" or "advanced" or "intelligent." They only drag us down to the level of Neanderthals, albeit ones wearing tailored suits.

Our knuckle-dragging ancestors may have been too "uncivilized" to scrape their adversaries' brains off the glacial sheets once their clubs had done their work, but we are deemed far too civilized to leave behind us such a ghastly mess.

Instead, we neatly vaporize our foes with our technological instruments of death and delude ourselves that we flourish in a "modern civilization."

Nothing within us has changed.

Nothing.

↩

*An eye for an eye will make
the whole world blind.*

—MAHATMA GANDHI

In wars invoked by zealots of one religion, they (misguidedly) believe that they are promised salvation if they destroy all enemies who do not believe in their god.

We in the West dismiss this belief as uncivilized, barbarian, heathen.

Then, the leader of the world's most powerful nation invokes *his* god's "will and divine guidance" in his effort to assassinate a despot—at the cost of thousands of innocent civilian lives (more than 20,000 at the last count). He brands the invasion of a sovereign nation as a "crusade" and declares war in the name of *his* god.

They kill us in the name of their god. We kill them in the name of ours.

And God weeps.

Has anyone stopped to wonder whether the One loving Creator of the Universe would

We have just enough religion to make us hate, but not enough to make us love one another.

—Jonathan Swift

encourage, let alone command, his creations to annihilate each other?

Is this the height to which our much-touted "intelligence" has evolved?

Common sense alone should shake us from these sectarian stupors and pry open our eyes.

*Being religious means asking
passionately the question of the
meaning of our existence and
being willing to receive answers,
even if the answers hurt.*

—Paul Tillich

↩

CHAPTER 3

Sanity

Is it not time to awaken and wash away this incendiary religious war-paint that spurs us to these ceaseless, ever-mounting cycles of destruction?

Is it not time we shed our partisan liturgical incantations and begin the quiet *inward* journey to find harmony and oneness with the Divine universal Force, the "Deathless Reality", that dwells within all sentient beings?

Recognizing the wispy intellectual roots of many of our dogmatic religious assumptions

Religions are all alike—founded
on fables and mythologies.

—THOMAS JEFFERSON

and customs; rationally examining them, and then jettisoning the ones that don't make sense would certainly help us begin the journey.

↭

For instance, would it be unreasonable to conclude that God—the Creator of the Cosmos, with its endless, fathomless sea of galaxies—is unlikely to have "personally" appointed the motley array of religious brokers and inter-pleaders on this planet, who claim to serve on His behalf?

Would it be ignorant to deduce that God is unlikely to have "personally" sanctioned the plethora of agencies and scriptures that usurp His name with such cavalier abandon?

Would it be unintelligent to surmise that God did not personally order the litany of taboos and rituals that followers of all religions so blindly obey?

*Today the god hypothesis has
ceased to be scientifically tenable...
and its abandonment often brings
a deep sense of relief. Many people
assert that this abandonment
of the god hypothesis means the
abandonment of all religion and
all moral sanctions. This is simply
not true. But it does mean, once
our relief at jettisoning an outdated
piece of ideological furniture is
over, that we must construct
some thing to take its place.*

—SIR JULIAN HUXLEY

Regardless of the religion involved, would not many of the decrees that are said to be God's word evaporate upon intelligent analysis?

Besides defying logic, some of these beliefs are an affront to the very intelligence and powers of reasoning God has bestowed on His creations.

↤

To wit, is it plausible that the Creator of the Universe would arbitrarily forbid a specific group of inhabitants of a speck of cosmic dust, floating at the edge of some obscure galaxy, from killing a particular breed of dumb animal (while permitting its meat to be relished by virtually everyone else)?

Is it conceivable that the Almighty would just as mysteriously order another group of denizens of this microscopic habitat to

*The idea that Jesus is the only
way to God or that only those who
have been washed in the blood
of Christ are ever to be listed
among the saved, has become
anathema and even dangerous
in our shrinking world.*
—EPISCOPAL BISHOP JOHN SPONG

rigidly avoid the meat of yet another beast, while allowing *its* flesh to flourish as a delicacy elsewhere? (Even that of clean, corn-fed specimens is verboten—but this very group is inexplicably permitted to gorge on prawns, crabs and the like that feed on feces?)

Is it probable that God would command that yet another group of inhabitants of this speck of stellar dust avoid all physical toil on one specific day of every week? (While living on a parcel of real estate that He allegedly bestowed *personally* on this clearly favored group?)

Is it credible that the compassionate Creator would summarily banish to "hell"—for eternity, no less—all those "heathens" who have not been "saved" and "born again" by hearing and accepting His alleged teachings disseminated through yet another branch of His curious array of messengers? (Even if the hapless souls

*The day will come when the
mystical generation of Jesus by
the Supreme Being in the womb
of a virgin, will be classed with
the fable of the generation of
Minerva in the brain of Jupiter.*

—THOMAS JEFFERSON

so cruelly sentenced lived pristinely virtuous lives, but committed the only sin of living too far away to be saved and enlightened by these mortal couriers?)

Is it likely that God literally dispatched His "only son" to this nondescript cosmic speck to set our species straight, thereby unfairly depriving the myriad other beings populating the rest of His Universe of like spiritual counsel? (This is a sad misinterpretation indeed, considering that the great spiritual teacher concerned said nothing of the sort. What he *did* say is that we are *all* God's children.)

Can one seriously entertain the possibility that it was God who was aboard the craft made of "glowing metal," that an ancient prophet saw "descending from the heavens with flashing lightning and surrounded by brilliant light;" and which utilized a strange "wheel

It may be that religion is dead,
and if it is, we had better know
it and set ourselves to try to
discover other sources of moral
strength before it is too late.

—Pearl S. Buck

intersecting a wheel" to traverse the ground after it had landed?

If God gadded about in a metallic spacecraft (one with a motive undercarriage, no less), could He be relied on to reach the infinitely distant corners of the Cosmos to tend to his scattered flock?

Surely, any sentient being of this age with a modicum of intellectual discernment would dismiss these beliefs as ludicrous after gazing up at the stars on a clear night and pondering the incomprehensible beauty of the Infinite?

Quite simply, one can either choose to see through this fog and be free, or wallow in it and be enslaved.

And therein lies the problem.

The Church says that the Earth is
flat, but I know that it is round.
For I have seen the shadow on the
moon and I have more faith in
the Shadow than in the Church.

—FERDINAND MAGELLAN

✑

CHAPTER 4

Blind Faith

Many "believers" are programmed from birth never to pollute their "faith" with their God-given powers of reason. The individual *inward* pursuit of Truth, and belief in a singular, nameless, universal Creator invites only rebuke, or some leprotic moniker such as "heathen", "atheist", "infidel" or "New Age nut." (It also causes empty collection plates, but that's another matter.)

Free thinkers who reflect on the mysteries of life and meditate in the sea of Universal

Real knowledge is to know the

extent of one's ignorance.

—Confucius

Consciousness present the greatest threat to the survival of religious myths. They are viewed by the various religions as the most diabolical form of heresy extant.

For example, to virtually every adherent of every known religion, such independent thinkers conjure visions of "the devil's work." That these "infidels" love, revere and worship God with all their being—albeit *sans* the dogma—seems not to matter a whit.

Fear is the mechanism of control that religions employ (subliminally, in this age) to ensure that their flocks never wander astray and spawn such dangerous iconoclastic agitators.

And blind, unquestioning "faith" is the euphemistic warrant waved in the faces of the believers as God's personal guarantee that reason and good judgment can now safely be tossed out the window.

*The further the spiritual evolution
of mankind advances, the more
certain it seems to me that the path
to genuine religiosity does not lie
through blind faith, but through
striving after rational knowledge.*

—ALBERT EINSTEIN

Blind faith is fear masquerading as truth. Fear, guilt, and condemnation form the bars of the religious prisons in which we have been trapped since the beginning of time.

Even after millennia of evolutionary intellectual growth, the seeds of fear and guilt implicit in the doctrines of our various religions continue to keep man's blinders firmly buckled.

And his furnaces of fury amply fueled.

It is a tragedy that generation upon generation, millennia upon millennia, religious man is conditioned from birth never to question, but always to obey the rules passed down to him by his forebears.

It is a sad commentary on the human condition that when it comes to spiritual matters, most people are afraid to think, question, or analyze independently in their hearts on a clean sheet devoid of dogma—even though

After long searches, here and there, in temples and in churches, in earths and in heavens, at last you come back, completing the circle from where you started, to your own soul, and find that He, for whom you have been seeking all over the world, for whom you have been weeping and praying in churches and temples, on whom you were looking as the mystery of all mysteries, shrouded in the clouds, is the nearest of the near, in your own self, the reality of your life, body and soul.

—SATHYA SAI BABA

virtually all spiritual teachers have urged their students to seek the Truth *within*.

Jesus said, "The kingdom of God is within you."

The Mahabharata urges devotees to "seek the Truth within oneself."

The Sufis, the mystics of Islam, have a verse that reads, "I searched for God and found only myself. I searched for myself and found only God."

The Buddha preached, "Do not ever accept something as Truth because someone said it is true...ask the Presence of God within your heart to allow you to clearly perceive only the Truth that will set you free. "

But, regardless of these consistent and compelling messages, our religious indoctrination of fear causes us to embrace, verbatim, scriptures written by ordinary men while

*People will do anything, no
matter how absurd, in order to
avoid facing their own soul.*

—CARL GUSTAV JUNG

ignoring the deeper Truths preached by the Masters.

Fear makes people refuse to think for themselves. They seek Truth everywhere but within their own souls. They ache for external dogmatic crutches to give them "strength." When the crutches are taken away, they feel lost and vulnerable. They feel a deep need to be herded by others who claim to be ordained instruments of God (and too many of whom, as we continue to see, merrily abuse helpless little children when God isn't looking).

The flocks are led to believe that without the salvation only religions and their self-appointed agents can provide, they would not only be lost in the wilderness, but also damned to boot.

And so it is that whichever "religion" one elects to examine, the docile actions of its

Among all my patients in the
second half of life...there has
not been one whose problem in
the last resort was not that of
finding a religious outlook on life.

—CARL JUNG

followers are ostensibly motivated by "faith," when in truth they are rooted in fear—the wrath of God, fire and brimstone, denial of a visa to heaven…

And so these myths endure, and are perpetuated through successive generational herds of "believers" who are similarly indoctrinated into lives of fearful obedience.

Thus snugly cocooned in their safe religious bubbles, each oozing its own soothing, sectarian dogmatic salve, the faithful are then promised their due rewards—heaven, nirvana, paradise…

So inspired, each group then dutifully brutalizes the other in order to advance its own superiority in accordance with the edicts of its own proprietary god.

*In the matter of religion, people
eagerly fasten their eyes on the
difference between their own
creed and yours; whilst the
charm of the study is in finding
the agreements and identities in
all the religions of humanity.*

—RALPH WALDO EMERSON

✑

CHAPTER 5

Commonality

The fundamental misunderstandings about the "differences" between religions become easier to grasp when one awakens to the fact that all religions essentially preach the same core tenet.

Take, for example, what Jesus exhorted in his Sermon on the Mount: "Therefore all things whatsoever ye would that men should do to you, do ye even so to them."

The Buddha gently counseled his devotees: "Hurt not others with that which pains yourself."

Religions are many and diverse,
but reason and goodness are one.

—ELBERT HUBBARD

Confucius impressed upon the minds of his followers: "What you do not want done to yourself, do not do to others."

The Qur'an of the Muslims admonishes, "No one of you is a believer until he loves for his brother what he loves for himself."

In Judaism the Torah instructs, "And thou shalt love thy neighbor as thyself."

The Hitopadesa of the Hindus proclaims, "Good people proceed while considering that what is best for others is best for themselves."

↬

When you recognize the similarity of these various precepts, the singularity of the Creator becomes obvious. Even when God speaks of wickedness, His loving kindness and compassion shine through all religions with indivisible coherence.

All...religions show the same disparity between belief and practice, and each is safe till it tries to exclude the rest. Test each sect by its best or its worst as you will, by its high-water mark of virtue or its low-water mark of vice. But falsehood begins when you measure the ebb of any other religion against the flood-tide of your own. There is a noble and a base side to every history.

—Thomas Wentworth Higginson

Jesus' God, "makes His sun rise on the wicked and on the good, and sends rain to the righteous and to the unrighteous."

Krishna's God showers His blessings upon, "all those who trust Me, even the lowest of the low—criminals, prostitutes, beggars, slaves…"

The Tao Te Ching says, "the Master welcomes both saints and sinners."

The messages of all these sacred scripts are virtually identical. Surely they all emanate from the same fount of Divine Universal Wisdom?

Where, then, lie the differences between religions?

The "differences" lie only in the polymorphic interpretations of man.

If we are to rise above the religious fray, we must learn to part these segregating doctrinal curtains and behold the face of the universal One.

Ever since I was a small child,
I've believed there was life
out there. When I look at the
magnitude of the universe, with
its billions of stars, I believe that
if life developed here on Earth, it
must have developed elsewhere.
We simply can't be unique. I
really don't think we're the most
intelligent life-form in the universe.

—DR. CLAIRE PARKINSON, NASA
SCIENTIST, AND WINNER OF 2001
EXCEPTIONAL SERVICE MEDAL

↩

CHAPTER 6

We Are Not Alone

The shortest path to sanity, and wisdom, would be to realize that we are not alone in the Universe. This knowledge could throw open doors to new, heretofore unimagined perspectives and spawn entirely new ways of thinking.

However, to most people, the idea of other intelligent beings in the universe throws up a thicket of barriers; it raises disconcerting questions that fall outside the comforting confines of their religious texts. I have known many deeply religious individuals who slammed

After a year of scrutiny of highly unconventional phenomena credibly reported from all parts of this country and, and from most of the entire world, I have been driven to consider possibilities that I'd ordinarily not give a moment's thought to in my own personal brand of orthodoxy. On the basis of an intensive study of the question, I believe that the extraterrestrial-intelligence hypothesis must now be given extremely serious scientific attention.

—Dr. James McDonald, Professor of Physics, University of Chicago; advisor to the National Science Foundation, The Office of Naval Research, and the National Academy of Sciences

down their mental barricades and denounced even tentative peeks into the "unknown" as heresy. Others have nervously attempted to intellectualize at the fringes of the concept, but refused to discuss or think about deeper issues and their ramifications.

To an open, curious mind, however, the existence of extraterrestrial life is not only possible: it is irresistibly logical, entirely reasonable, and altogether probable.

Just as the oceans of our own planet teem with billions of extraordinarily dissimilar creatures, so must God's "celestial ocean"—the infinite Universe—contain countless planets bearing intelligent beings of unimaginable variety.

Surely it is feasible that some of these beings nurture their *own* unique "religious" beliefs, and cherish their own unique views of what they consider to be *their* Creator? And perhaps,

There is no doubt in my mind, after 37 years of study and investigation that the evidence is overwhelming…there are no acceptable arguments against [extraterrestrial vehicles], only people who either haven't studied the relevant data or have a strong will not to believe that Earth is at the bottom of the heap sociologically and technologically in our galactic neighborhood.

—STANTON FRIEDMAN, NUCLEAR PHYSICIST AND RESEARCHER WHO HAS PROVIDED WRITTEN TESTIMONY TO CONGRESSIONAL HEARINGS AND THE UNITED NATIONS

like us, might even jealously claim that *they* have been created in His image, whatever that image might be—Reptilian? Ornithological? Botanical? Aquatic?

Does this mean, then, that a motley consortium of gods governs the Universe, each one presiding over his own cosmic sector?

The notion is absurd.

Could any open-minded person continue to believe that humans are the center of all creation upon viewing the Hubble Telescope's awe-inspiring photographs of the boundless cosmological vistas that lie within a mere pinpoint of the visible Universe?

If such spectacular visions of the cosmos fail to open our minds, perhaps more intellectual concepts can do so. One such is the famous Green Bank Equation.

In 1961, a group of preeminent astronomers

*The phenomenon reported is
something real, and not visionary
or fictitious. There are objects
approximating the shape of a
disk, of such appreciable size
as to appear to be as large as a
man-made aircraft. The reported
operating characteristics such
as extreme rates of climb,
maneuverability...and actions that
must be considered evasive when
sighted or contacted by friendly
aircraft and radar, lend belief to
the possibility that the objects
are controlled either manually,
automatically or remotely.*

—GENERAL NATHAN F. TWINING, COMMANDING-
GENERAL OF THE AIR MATERIEL COMMAND, IN A
REPORT CLASSIFIED TOP SECRET DATED SEPTEMBER
23, 1947, ADDRESSED TO BRIGADIER GENERAL
GEORGE SCHULGEN, CHIEF OF THE AIR INTELLIGENCE
REQUIREMENTS DIVISION AT THE PENTAGON

and physicists convened at the Green Bank Observatory in West Virginia to determine the probability of extraterrestrial life in our Milky Way Galaxy. The resulting Green Bank Equation yields the probable number of technically advanced civilizations in our galaxy as a function of other astronomical, biological, and psychological factors. It suggests that there could be as many as *50 million* different civilizations in *our galaxy alone,* not to mention the trillions of other galaxies peppered across the known universe.

Sir James Jeans, the distinguished British astrophysicist, estimated the known Universe to be about one trillion times as big as the area of space visible through our most powerful telescopes (those available in the 1930s). He compared the total number of galaxies in our universe to the total number of grains of sand on all the seashores of the world.

Unknown objects are operating under intelligent control... It is imperative that we learn where they come from and what their purpose is...It is time for the truth to be brought out in open Congressional hearings. Behind the scenes, high-ranking Air Force officers are soberly concerned about these unidentified vehicles. But through official secrecy and ridicule, many citizens are led to believe the unknown flying objects are nonsense. I urge immediate Congressional action...

—ADMIRAL ROSCOE HILLENKOETTER, FORMER DIRECTOR OF THE CIA (1947-50) AND PACIFIC COMMANDER OF INTELLIGENCE DURING WORLD WAR II, IN A SIGNED STATEMENT DATED AUGUST 22, 1960, SENT TO CONGRESS

This mind-boggling analogy deserves emphasis: Jeans referred not to mere planets, nor even solar systems, but to *Galaxies*, each of which contains *hundreds of billions* of solar systems similar to ours.

↩

The odds overwhelmingly support the existence of life elsewhere, but these are probabilities the average person dares not think about. Its implications are far too problematic. (It's interesting that these very people have no qualms about the validity of death sentences based on DNA evidence, for which the odds of a match are less than those in favor of the existence of other intelligent life in the universe.)

Denial, and intransigence in the face of overwhelming evidence can conspire to form impenetrable barriers. Given the egocentric nature

More than 10,000 sightings have been reported, the majority of which cannot be accounted for by any 'scientific' explanation. I am convinced that these objects do exist and that they are not manufactured by any nation on earth. I can therefore see no alternative to accepting the theory that they come from some extraterrestrial source. [These] visitors might have come bent solely on scientific discovery and might regard us with the dispassionate aloofness that we might regard insects found beneath an upturned stone.

—AIR CHIEF MARSHAL LORD HUGH DOWDING, COMMANDER-IN-CHIEF OF RAF FIGHTER COMMAND DURING THE BATTLE OF BRITAIN. DOWDING'S REMARKABLE CAREER ENDED IN CONTROVERSY AND INTRIGUE WHEN HE WAS DISMISSED FROM HIS POST IN THE SAME YEAR DESPITE HIS ROLE IN WINNING THE CRUCIAL BATTLE OF BRITAIN

of our species and the immovable mindset of deeply religious (and ultra-nationalistic) people, acceptance of extraterrestrial life could be an impossible leap of faith for many. It falls too far outside our miniscule frame of reference.

Nonetheless, that our species will make such a leap is as inevitable as our ancestors' leaps across similar paradigm-shattering chasms. We now know that the stars were not ornamentally hung in the firmament by a phalanx of capricious gods; the Earth is not the center of the universe; the sun does not revolve around our planet; you will not fall off the edge of the Earth if you sail too far towards the horizon; heavier-than-air flight is possible; and a rocket can function in a vacuum. Slowly and inexorably, truth marches forward as ignorance and denial wither and fall by the wayside.

Of course, thousands of years of mental

I can assure you that flying saucers,
given that they exist, are not
constructed by any power on earth.
—PRESIDENT HARRY S. TRUMAN, APRIL 4, 1950,
AT A WHITE HOUSE PRESS CONFERENCE

...In the firm belief that the American public
deserves a better explanation than that
thus far given by the Air Force, I strongly
recommend that there be a committee
investigation of the UFO phenomena. I think
we owe it to the people to establish credibility
regarding UFOs and to produce the greatest
possible enlightenment on this subject.
—PRESIDENT GERALD FORD, IN A LETTER HE SENT AS
A CONGRESSMAN TO L. MENDEL RIVERS, CHAIRMAN OF
THE ARMED SERVICES COMMITTEE, 28 MARCH 1966

I am convinced that UFOs exist because
I've seen one... One thing's for sure, I'll
never make fun of people who say they've
seen unidentified objects in the sky.
—PRESIDENT JIMMY CARTER, MAY 1976

conditioning and Earth-centered thinking cannot be altered overnight. As Max Planck, the Nobel Prize-winning physicist, observed, "An important idea rarely makes its way by gradually winning over and converting its opponents; what does happen is that the opponents gradually die out."

How many of Copernicus's peers and contemporaries had to die before the primitive myth that the sun revolved around the Earth could be buried? So it will be with those who resist the idea of extraterrestrial intelligence. And, as with every other groundbreaking discovery, the day will certainly dawn when more people accept it than not. The transition has already begun, and this shift in thinking is far more prevalent (outside dogmatic religious circles, of course) than is generally known.

But until we *all* perceive the awesome vast-

I did have occasion in 1951 [while assigned to the 86th Fighter Group in Munich, Germany] to have two days of observation of many flights of UFOs flying in formation over Europe …we tried to get close to them, but they were able to change direction faster than our fighters. I believe that these are extraterrestrial vehicles visiting this planet from other planets, which are obviously more advanced than we are here on earth.

—GORDON COOPER, MERCURY
ASTRONAUT, ADDRESSING A
MEETING OF THE SPECIAL POLITICAL
COMMITTEE OF THE UNITED NATIONS
GENERAL ASSEMBLY IN 1978

ness of the cosmos; collectively accept the reality that countless intelligent life forms inhabit the universe; and know that one universal God is the creator of All, we will not awaken to the spiritual unity of our species. Only this pivotal realization can bring a lasting peace to our little planet ravaged and shredded by ignorant thinking.

For those willing to explore the ancient sacred texts of the world without religious prejudice, there is an abundance of evidence that not only asserts God's omnipotent unity, but also describes the reality of other life-sustaining worlds.

The scriptures of one religion express such a reality by describing God as, "The Unified Cosmic Body that encompasses *all worlds...with their countless billions of life-forms..."*

God proclaims in another ancient text: "There is nothing more fundamental than I...

*I was testing a P-51 fighter in
Minneapolis when I spotted this
object. I was at about 10,000 feet
on a nice, bright, sunny afternoon.
I thought the object was a kite,
then realized that no kite is gonna
[sic] fly that high...as soon as I got
behind the darn thing...it looked
like a saucer, a disk...I tracked
it for a little way, and all of a
sudden the damn thing just took
off. It pulled about a 45-degree
climbing turn and accelerated
and just flat disappeared.*

—DONALD SLAYTON, MERCURY ASTRONAUT,
DESCRIBING A UFO ENCOUNTER IN 1951
TO INTERVIEWER PAUL LEVY IN 1979

all worlds, all beings, are strung upon me like pearls on a single thread…"

A verse in the holy book of another religion states: "And among God's signs is the creation of the *heaven and the Earth, and the living creatures He has scattered through them."*

The question we should ask ourselves is not, "Is the existence of other intelligent life forms in the universe possible?" *Au contraire,* we should be asking, "Is not the *absence* of other life forms *impossible?"*

↢

Our path to accepting these new ideas will not be without obstacles. Even with all our technological advances and exalted missions into space, as a species, we languish like the proverbial frogs in the well. Despite our egoistic preoccupation with Planet Earth, the truth is that

*I am aware that hundreds of
military and airline pilots, airport
personnel, astronomers, missile
trackers and other competent
observers have reported sightings of
UFOs. I am also aware that many
of these UFOs have been reported
maneuvering in formation, and
that many were simultaneously
tracked by radar. It is my opinion
that UFOs…are devices under
intelligent control. Their speeds,
maneuvers and other technical
evidence prove them superior
to any known aircraft or space
devices now produced on earth.*

—COLONEL JOSEPH J. BRYAN III, FOUNDER AND
ORIGINAL CHIEF OF THE CIA'S PSYCHOLOGICAL
WARFARE STAFF, AND FORMER SPECIAL ASSISTANT
TO THE SECRETARY OF THE AIR FORCE, AS
WELL AS AVIATION ADVISOR TO NATO

we are merely a curious, almost inconsequential microcosm floating in the boundless vastness of the Universe. Our own innate curiosity has yet to awaken, and our egos yet to concede, that we are physically—but not spiritually—insignificant in the grand cosmic scheme.

↬

Our minds will only *truly* open when we encounter intelligent beings far more advanced than we are from elsewhere in the cosmos, who may bear little, if any, likeness—chemically, elementally, dimensionally—to our humanoid selves, and who have transcended our primal and barbarous proclivities for greed, violence and domination.

Such a discovery will finally shatter this planet's religious, ethnic, and national barriers in one stupendously seminal revelatory instant.

They are space ships from another, or more than
one, solar system. ...They possibly are manned by
intelligent observers who are members of a race that
may have been investigating our earth for centuries.
Today we cannot produce machines that fly as UFOs
do. They are flying by means of artificial fields of
gravity. This would explain the sudden changes
of direction... They produce high-tension electric
charges to push the air out of their path...and strong
magnetic fields to influence the ionized air at higher
altitudes...this would explain their luminosity...
[also] it would explain the noiselessness of UFO
flight. ...This assumption also explains the strong
electrical and magnetic effects sometimes, but
not always, observed in the vicinity of UFOs.

—PROFESSOR HERMANN OBERTH, PHYSICIST, GERMAN
ROCKET PIONEER AND "FATHER OF ROCKETRY AND
MODERN ASTRONAUTICS." DR. OBERTH WAS INVITED BY
DR. WERNHER VON BRAUN (WHO ALSO BELIEVED UFOS
ARE EXTRATERRESTRIAL VEHICLES) TO GO TO THE UNITED
STATES, WHERE HE WORKED ON ROCKETS WITH THE
ARMY BALLISTIC MISSILE AGENCY, AND LATER, NASA

Despite our superficial physical differences—Negroid, Caucasian, Oriental—we will suddenly see that we are all members of the species *homo sapiens*. Despite our religious differences—Christian, Hindu, Catholic, Muslim, Jewish—it will crystallize that we are all children of the One loving Creator of the Universe.

This sweeping, macroscopic perspective of the multiplicity of life in the cosmos will instantly debunk our self-aggrandizing posture of superiority as "the chosen ones" of God's Universe, and lead us to conclude that our petty earthly religious prejudices, divisions, and squabbles—especially those proclaimed "in the name of God"—are groundless, shallow, pitiful, and laughable.

Suggested reading on extraterrestrial intelligence: *Above Top Secret,* Timothy Good; *Top Secret/MAJIC,* Stanton T. Friedman; *Extraterrestrials In Biblical Prophecy,* G. Cope Schellhorn; *The Day After Roswell,* Colonel Philip J. Corso; *Abduction,* John E. Mack, MD; *The Flying Saucers Are Real,* Major Donald Keyhoe.

*Much evidence tells us they have been tracked
by radar; so, UFOs are real and they may come
from outer space...the dream of our pilots is to
acquire the technique of gravity-control, capable
of perfectly free maneuverability. Photographs and
various materials show scientifically that there
are more advanced people piloting the saucers...*

—GENERAL KANSHI ISHIKAWA, CHIEF OF AIR STAFF
OF JAPAN'S AIR SELF-DEFENSE FORCE; 1967

*Radar is not subject to optical illusions.
Radar echoes are due to solid objects...*

—AIR MINISTER BRIGADIER OTÁVIO JÚLIO MOREIRA
LIMA, BRAZILIAN AIR FORCE; AT THE PRESS CONFERENCE
FOLLOWING A BRAZILIAN DEFENSE CENTER ALERT
THAT SCRAMBLED THREE F5-E TIGER JETS AND THREE
MIRAGE III JETS IN PURSUIT OF A UFO. ALL SIX PILOTS
OBSERVED THE UFO ON THEIR RADAR SETS BEFORE THE
CRAFT EXECUTED AN INSTANTANEOUS 180-DEGREE
TURN WHILE TRAVELING AT OVER 1,000 KILOMETERS
PER HOUR AND DISAPPEARED VERTICALLY; MAY 1986

As far as my staff is concerned, we believe implicitly that the unexplained UFOs are from some civilization beyond our planet.

—AIR COMMODORE DAVID THORNE, DIRECTOR GENERAL OF OPERATIONS, AIR FORCE OF ZIMBABWE, REFERRING TO AN INCIDENT IN WHICH TWO HAWK JETS WERE SCRAMBLED FROM THORNHILL AIR BASE TO INTERCEPT A RADAR-VERIFIED UFO, WHICH, WHEN APPROACHED BY THE JETS, SUDDENLY ACCELERATED FROM A HOVER AT 7,000 FEET TO AN ALTITUDE OF 70,000 FEET IN LESS THAN ONE MINUTE; 1985

It appears to be a metallic object…tremendous in size…directly ahead and slightly above…I am trying to close in for a better look.

—THE LAST WORDS OF US AIR FORCE CAPTAIN THOMAS MANTELL, FLYING A P-51 MUSTANG, AFTER HE WAS REQUESTED BY THE CONTROL TOWER AT GODMAN AFB, KENTUCKY, TO INVESTIGATE A UFO DETECTED ON RADAR. HIS AIRCRAFT CRASHED NEAR FRANKLIN, KENTUCKY KILLING MANTELL; 1948. THE UFO WAS WITNESSED BY MORE THAN 100 PEOPLE INCLUDING STATE POLICE AND MILITARY POLICE AT FORT KNOX; THE WALNUT-SHAPED CRAFT WAS ESTIMATED TO BE OVER 300 FEET IN DIAMETER

*We have stacks of reports of flying saucers. We
take them seriously when you consider we have lost
many men and planes trying to intercept them.*

—General Benjamin Chidlaw, former
Commanding General of Air Defense Command,
to researcher Robert Gardner in 1953

*On the basis of my official research and investigation
into UFO sightings and reports of alien contact, I am
personally convinced that intelligent extraterrestrials
are visiting Earth. I say this on the basis of the
data available to me at the Ministry of Defense,
both in terms of the historic records and the several
hundred new cases that I investigated each year.
There was a hard core of cases that defied any
conventional explanation and involved craft capable
of speeds and maneuvers beyond the capabilities of
our own technology. I was particularly interested
in UFO sightings that could be correlated by radar
and in reports where the witnesses were military
personnel; such cases were directly responsible for
my gradual conversion from skeptic to believer.*

—Nick Pope, official government
researcher on UFOs for British Ministry
of Defense, and renowned author

The fact that since 1946 numerous persons in all countries have made detailed reports of events they regard as strange, mysterious, sometimes even terrifying, deserves attention. While many of the reports can be traced to natural events, we intend to demonstrate that, after the inevitable errors and the obvious hoaxes are eliminated, the reports reveal common characteristics, possess a high degree of internal coherence, and appear to be the result of the witnesses' exposure to a set of unusual circumstances. Skeptics, who flatly deny the existence of any unexplained phenomenon in the name of 'rationalism,' are among the primary contributors to the rejection of science by the public. People are not stupid and they know very well when they have seen something out of the ordinary. When a so-called expert tells them the object must have been the moon or a mirage, he is really teaching the public that science is impotent or unwilling to pursue the study of the unknown.

—JACQUES VALLEE, PHD, ASTROPHYSICIST; CO-
DEVELOPER, AT THE UNIVERSITY OF TEXAS, OF THE
FIRST COMPUTER-BASED MAP OF MARS FOR NASA

*A purely psychological explanation is ruled
out ... The American Air Force (despite its
contradictory statements)...consider the
observations to be real...However, the "disks" do
not behave in accordance with physical laws but
as though without weight, and they show signs
of intelligent guidance by quasi-human pilots.*

—Dr. Carl Gustav Jung, Pioneer
of psychiatry, 1954

*From observers who range from illiterate peasants
in Argentina and Spain to people with PhDs in other
countries...there have been tens of thousands of
sightings and encounters, physical results, and of the
latter, by people whose evidence on any other subject
would be accepted without question. ...I claim that
the charge that there is a cover-up is thereby proved.
What I admit defeats me is a plausible reason for it.*

—Admiral of the Fleet, Lord Hill-Norton,
GCB, Chief of Defense Staff, Ministry
of Defense, Great Britain (1971-73)

*[The reason for the official silence] is to maintain a
workable stability among the nations of the world
and for them, in turn, to retain institutional control
over their respective populations. Thus, for these
governments to admit that there are beings from
outer space…with mentalities and technological
capabilities obviously far superior to ours, could,
once fully perceived by the average person,
erode the foundations of the earth's traditional
power structure. Political and legal systems,
religions, economic and social institutions could
all soon become meaningless in the mind of the
public. The national oligarchical establishments,
even civilization as we know it, could collapse
into anarchy. Such extreme conclusions are not
necessarily valid, but they probably accurately
reflect the fears of the "ruling classes" of the
major nations, whose leaders (particularly
those in the intelligence business) have always
advocated excessive governmental secrecy as
being necessary to preserve "national security."*

—VICTOR MARCHETTI, FORMER EXECUTIVE ASSISTANT
TO THE DEPUTY DIRECTOR, AND SPECIAL ASSISTANT
TO THE EXECUTIVE DIRECTOR OF THE CIA; IN HIS
BOOK, HOW THE CIA VIEWS THE UFO PHENOMENON

*Astronauts, Physicists, World
leaders, Generals, Admirals,
Intelligence Chiefs, Scientists,
Psychiatrists, Test pilots...*

*They all believe in intelligent
life elsewhere in the Universe.*

Are they all wrong?

*Were an Asiatic to ask me for a
definition of Europe, I should be
forced to answer him: It is that
part of the world which is haunted
by the incredible delusion that
man was created out of nothing,
and that his present birth is
his first entrance into life.*

—ARTHUR SCHOPENHAUER

‹⊕›

CHAPTER 7

Journey of the Soul

There is another path—albeit a deeper, more "exotic" one—which might help us realize the folly and futility of murdering our fellow humans, whether or not we do so "in the name of God."

It is not the purpose of this book to engage in a deep discussion of this particularly contentious subject. But given the sheer weight of inductive reasoning and overwhelming evidence in support of it, a brief excursion into the fascinating realm of reincarnation is in

Do not seek to follow in the footsteps of the men of old. Seek what they sought.

—MATSUO BASHO

order. If we are to liberate our minds from the archaic bonds of outmoded thinking, it would be appropriate here to examine not only what is probable in the realm of human rebirth, but also that which resonates with the weight of truth based on human experience.

↔

As nature and science inarguably attest, the Universe is the epitome of perfect order and harmony—what Pythagoras referred to as the "music of the spheres," or, as David Bohm, one of the leading quantum physicists of our age called it, the "Implicate Order." The theory of the Implicate Order is an ultra-holistic cosmic view that connects everything with everything else in perfect harmony.

In an immaculate system like Nature, nothing happens by accident. Absolutely nothing

Our birth is but a sleep and
a forgetting; The Soul that
rises with us, our life's Star,
Hath had elsewhere its setting.
And cometh from afar.
—WILLIAM WORDSWORTH

is left to chance. The orbital velocity of an electron around its nucleus is as precisely computed and sustained by Nature as that of a planet around its sun. An accidental decay of either would lead to catastrophic consequences, but Nature hums along with perfectly structured precision, missing nary a beat. The Universe is the quintessence of perfect order, the work of the Great Unseen Force.

Equally true and inviolate are the laws of cause and effect that bind and sustain this unimaginably precise, impossibly flawless system.

Another truth that we have come to accept is that of God's impartiality towards His living creations. Now that we have discarded the capricious gods of yore who flung everything from floods to famine at the wretched, we largely agree that the Creator doesn't play favorites. Surely, His is the ultimate level playing field?

*The soul comes from without
into the human body, as
into a temporary abode, and
it goes out of it anew as it
passes into other habitations,
for the soul is immortal.*

—RALPH WALDO EMERSON

It is also true that many people—mainly those who dismiss reincarnation as nonsense—believe that the souls of newborn infants are faultless, pure, and innocent. (Since they've just been freshly minted, goes the reasoning, they've yet to commit "sin.")

Now, if all of the above is true, we must ask the question, "Why would an excruciatingly ordered and impartial Creator cause one innocent baby to be born to a syphilitic prostitute in a slum in Calcutta, and then, in an inexplicable act of magnanimity, cause another similarly faultless child to be born in a gilded chamber in Buckingham Palace?"

The only inference one can make from this cruelest of imbalances—the ultimate handicap—is that God is whimsical, petulant, and heartless.

But wouldn't such bizarrely capricious and

*All human beings go through a
previous life... Who knows how
many fleshly forms the heir of
heaven occupies before he can be
brought to understand the value
of that silence and solitude of
spiritual worlds?*

—HONORE BALZAC

erratic behavior fly in the face of God's precisely planned and structured Universe whose mechanisms reveal no bias or chance in their flawless functioning? Why would a Creator who is the epitome of balance, order, justice, and love be so rash, desultory, and mercurial when it comes to sending forth innocent souls into this physical plane of existence? The typical response from those wearing doctrinal blinders is, "God works in mysterious ways; it is not ours to question."

Reincarnation is the only rational explanation for various otherwise inexplicable elements of our lives and personalities. For instance, why does a young child show great musical talent when the parents have none? Why do children remember, to the smallest detail sometimes, a previous life in a strange land, as a member of an unknown family?

I know I am deathless. No doubt
I have died myself ten thousand
times before. I laugh at what you
call dissolution, and I know the
amplitude of time.

—WALT WHITMAN

And often even speak fluently in that foreign tongue?

Renowned Western psychiatrists and psychologists have documented thousands of such instances around the world. Indeed, these children's stories have often been empirically verified. (A notable work on the subject is *Twenty Cases Suggestive of Reincarnation* by Ian Stevenson, M.D. Dr. Stevenson is the former head of the Department of Psychiatry at the University of Virginia, and now is Director of the Division of Personality Studies at that university. He has devoted the last forty years to the scientific documentation of past life memories of children from all over the world, and has over 3,000 cases in his files. Many people, including skeptics and scholars, agree that these cases offer the best evidence yet for reincarnation. Dr. Harold Lief stated in the *Journal of Nervous*

My life often seemed to me like a story that has no beginning and no end. I had the feeling that I was an historical fragment, an excerpt for which the preceding and succeeding text was missing. I could well imagine that I might have lived in former centuries and there encountered questions I was not yet able to answer; that I had been born again because I had not fulfilled the task given to me.

—Dr. Carl Gustav Jung

and Mental Diseases, "Either Dr. Stevenson is making a colossal mistake, or he will be known as the Galileo of the 20th century.")

Why are we attracted to certain places or certain types of people? Why do some people seem wise beyond their years? These and many other questions can only be satisfactorily answered through a study of reincarnation.

A multitude of ancient scriptures tell us that we are not human beings having a spiritual experience, but rather, spiritual beings having a human experience. These teachings speak of the eternal, deathless nature of the soul and its journey to eventual perfection—union with God—through numerous cycles of death and rebirth. They compare our earthly incarnations to classrooms—opportunities to atone for past mistakes, to learn, and to advance up the spiritual ladder toward perfection.

*I am confident that there truly
is such a thing as living again,
that the living spring from
the dead, and that the souls of
the dead are in existence.*

—SOCRATES

It is evident that not everyone who lives by the sword always dies by the sword. Legions of villains throughout history have got away with their crimes. Millions of murderers, thieves, rapists, and the like have basked in comfort and luxury, even enjoyed perfect health, right up until their dying breaths. Did they get away with their crimes? If they did, how did they manage to beat the ageless system of cause and effect?

If these people did not escape Divine Justice, where and how will they atone for their transgressions? Do they pay for their crimes in "hell"? If so, for how long? Surely it could not be forever, as that would violate a cardinal law of Nature: a finite cause cannot produce an infinite effect. And should a pickpocket and a serial killer both receive the same hellish torment while there?

As long as you are not aware
of the continual law of Die and
Be Again, you are merely a
vague guest on a dark Earth.
—JOHANN WOLFGANG VON GOETHE

Or rather, is it possible that "hell" or "heaven" represents the conditions in each soul's next life here, in this "classroom" we call Earth, shared with other "classmates" to make atonement possible and purposeful?

There is abundant evidence in Nature of the seasonal "wheel of life and death." This observation caused Voltaire to pronounce, "It is no more surprising to be born once than to be born twice: everything in nature is resurrection." Given Nature's manner of functioning, doesn't reincarnation make more sense than an impish God who flippantly rolls the dice?

The truth is that more people in the world believe in reincarnation than do not. (Unfortunately, many of these must only be paying it lip service, since a true believer would find it impossible to cause harm to another.) Even in the United States, a Gallup poll a few years

The origin of the philosophy
of reincarnation is prehistoric.
It antedates antiquity
all over the world.

—E.D. WALKER

ago showed that nearly one in three Americans believes in some kind of reincarnation.

Almost all the ancient cultures and peoples of the world embrace reincarnation, or have embraced it at some time. Historically, Druids, Celts, Britons, Gallics, Platonists, Pythagoreans, Buddhists, Hindus, and many early Christians—including the apostles of Jesus Christ—have adhered to this doctrine. We can include the Inca and Mayan civilizations; the ancient Egyptians; the Roman poets Vergil, Lucretius, and Horatio; the Stoics, including Leonardo da Vinci; Madame Curie; and even Benjamin Franklin. Mozart was convinced that his genius derived from a past life. The Jewish Sohar, the famous Kabbalistic book, contains references to reincarnation, as do the Qur'an and the Mahabharata.

The list of brilliant thinkers throughout

I adopted the theory of reincarnation when I was 26. Genius is experience. Some seem to think that it is a gift or talent, but it is the fruit of long experience in many lives.

—Henry Ford

As far back as I can remember I have unconsciously referred to the experiences of previous existences… As the stars looked to me when I was a shepherd in Assyria, they look to me now as a New-Englander.

—Henry David Thoreau

history who taught the doctrine of rebirth is virtually endless. To name a few: Plato, Pythagoras, Origen, St. Augustine, Philo Judaeus, Paracelsus, Boehme, Spinoza, Leibniz, Schopenhauer, Goethe, Bruno, Kant, Blake, Schiller, Emerson, Thoreau, Whitman, Browning, Flaubert, Wagner, Tolstoy, Kipling, Sibelius, McTaggart, Gandhi...

Benjamin Franklin, one of the founding fathers of the United States, was such a firm believer that he wrote the following epitaph for himself, which was later published in the *New England Courant:* "The body of Benjamin Franklin, printer, like the cover of an old book, its Contents torn out and stripped of its lettering and gilding, lies here, food for worms. But the work shall not be lost; for it will, as he believed, appear once more in a new and more elegant edition, revised and corrected by the Author."

There is no death. How can there
be death if everything is part of
the Godhead? The soul never dies
and the body is never really alive.

—Isaac Bashevis Singer

Is it more than coincidence that Mr. Franklin's epitaph mirrors the 5,000-year-old Sanskrit text of the *Bhagavad-Gita,* which says: "As a man discards worn-out clothes to put on new and different ones, so the embodied self discards its worn-out bodies to take on other new ones"?

Many Christians reject reincarnation because it appears to conflict with their interpretation of Christian doctrines. But they are usually quite surprised to learn that reincarnation was a doctrine once held by many early Christians. The Gnostic Gospels attribute the following statement to Jesus: "Souls are poured from one into another of different kinds of bodies of the world."

Unfortunately, Christian belief in reincarnation was condemned and forbidden in 533 AD by the fifth ecumenical council in

But I tell you, Elijah has already come, and they did not recognize him, but have done to him everything they wished. In the same way the Son of Man is going to suffer at their hands. Then the disciples understood that he was talking to them about John the Baptist.

—JESUS, (MATTHEW 17:12, 13)

Constantinople, and all such references were excised from the Bible. But evidence remains in the Bible that Jesus taught this truth. Jesus affirmed to his disciples, in very explicit language, that John the Baptist was the reincarnation of the prophet Elijah. Throughout his ministry, Jesus taught people about the true resurrection—spiritual rebirth within a living person. (More Biblical evidence can be found in Herbert Puryear's outstanding book *Why Jesus Taught Reincarnation* and Dr. Quincy Howe, Jr.'s excellent book *Reincarnation For The Christian*.)

Lao Tse, considered the first philosopher of the Taoist school, said some 3,000 years ago, "The transformation toward eternal life is gradual...the heavy, gross energy of body, mind, and spirit must first be purified and uplifted..."

*No honest theologian therefore
can deny that his acceptance of
Jesus as Christ logically binds
every Christian to a belief in
reincarnation—in Elias case (who
was later John the Baptist) at least.*

—ROBERT GRAVES

In Islam, God speaks through a verse in the Qur'an: "And you were dead, and He brought you back to life. And He shall cause you to die, and shall bring you back to life, and in the end shall gather you unto Himself."

Suggestions of reincarnation are also common in the history of Judaism. Information about past lives is found throughout the Kabbalah, which, according to many Hebraic scholars, represents the hidden wisdom behind the scriptures. In the Zohar, one of the principal Kabbalistic texts, it is said, "The souls must reenter the absolute substance whence they have emerged. But to accomplish this, they must develop all the perfections, the germ of which is planted in them; and if they have not fulfilled this condition during one life, they must commence another, a third, and so forth, until they have acquired the condition which fits them for reunion with God."

*So as through a glass and
darkly, the age long strife I see,
Where I fought in many guises,
many names, but always me.*
—General George S. Patton

According to the *Universal Jewish Encyclopedia,* the Hasidic Jews hold similar beliefs.

Leo Tolstoy, who believed in the soul's immortality and rebirth, interjected a lively bit of logic and reverse thinking when he said, "The soul is immortal—well then, if I shall always live, I must have lived before, lived for a whole eternity."

Paragons of science and technology have spoken in support of the immortality of the soul. (This is not to say that such truths require mortal endorsement; as an ancient Vedic text reminds us, almost tongue-in-cheek, "whether or not one believes in reincarnation will not change the fact an iota.") Werner Von Braun, the preeminent rocket scientist, melded spirituality with science when he pronounced, "Everything science has taught me strengthens my belief in the continuity of our spiritual existence after

*When the physical organism
breaks up, the soul survives. It
then takes on another body.*

—PAUL GAUGUIN

death. I believe in an immortal soul. Science has proved that nothing disintegrates into nothingness. Life and soul, therefore, cannot disintegrate into nothingness, and so are immortal."

In spite of the laws of conservation of energy and matter that Von Braun, Einstein, and others have invoked in support of the immortality of the soul, scientific rejection of reincarnation continues, mainly on the strength of the supposed numerical improbabilities that it engenders. It is argued that because the Earth's human population has increased over the course of history, more people are currently living than have ever lived for the entire history of humankind. Thus, they argue, there would not be enough souls to fill these new bodies.

This line of reasoning presupposes that

*As we live through thousands of
dreams in our present life, so is
our present life only one of many
thousands of such lives which we
enter from the other more real
life and then return after death.
Our life is but one of the dreams
of that more real life, and so it is
endlessly, until the very last one,
the very real, the life of God.*

—Leo Tolstoy

intelligent life exists only on Earth, and that if we reincarnate, this planet and the human form are the soul's only available options. Unfortunately—as was explained in the previous chapter—this argument will continue to exist as long as the mind fails to break through its Earthbound anthropocentric barriers and awaken to the reality of a universe teeming with life.

Is it possible that some of us might have experienced prior incarnations in other physical environments—and even other forms? Is it conceivable, as many religious texts state, that our soul reincarnates on the physical plane again and again until it "graduates" from the "school" of physical life? Does it make sense that by choosing different bodies and different life experiences, the soul learns to view life from various perspectives—male or female, black or white, rich or poor, straight or gay,

*It is the secret of the world that all
things subsist and do not die, but
only retire a little from sight and
afterwards return again. Nothing
is dead; men feign themselves
dead, and endure mock funerals…
and there they stand looking out
of the window, sound and well,
in some strange new disguise.*

—RALPH WALDO EMERSON

for example? And that the soul carries these experiences into the next life, where we don't consciously remember them?

(Remembering past lives is another common point of contention; some argue that if the objective is to correct mistakes from a previous life, we should be able to remember these mistakes. However, ancient Tibetan and Vedic scriptures explain that we can only pass these "tests" honestly if we do not know how we failed them in the past. They also mention that conscious recollection of past lives would be too overwhelming.)

These scriptures claim that we often return to be with family or friends whom we know from a previous lifetime. Leading researchers such as Dr. Brian Weiss concur. Dr. Weiss is a *Phi Beta Kappa* graduate of Columbia University and Yale Medical School, and the former

Him that overcometh will I make

a pillar in the temple of my God,

and he shall go no more out.

BIBLE: REVELATIONS (3:12)
("OUT" IMPLYING OUT INTO THE
WORLD OF BIRTH AND DEATH)

chairman of the Department of Psychiatry at Mount Sinai Medical Center in Miami, Florida. His groundbreaking book *Many Lives, Many Masters* addresses the patterns of karma (cause and effect) that bring us into contact with those we have known before.

Our goals on Earth are to learn how to love, to feel compassion for other souls (especially those clothed in less fortunate fleshly garb), to achieve self-mastery, and to find our way home to The One, after which we "shall go no more out." Instead, too many of us are mired in greed, intolerance, selfishness, bigotry, and the like. Worse, through our national, ethnic, and religious chauvinism and our endless warmongering, we find ourselves drenched in the blood of our fellow travelers.

Opening our minds to this new way of thinking changes everything.

I cannot think of permanent enmity
between man and man, and
believing as I do in the theory of
reincarnation, I live in the hope
that if not in this birth, in some
other birth I shall be able to hug
all of humanity in friendly embrace.

—MAHATMA GHANDI

Can religious bigotry and racial animosity survive under the loving light of divine wisdom? For instance, would a Jew ever kill a Muslim if he knew he would likely reincarnate as a Muslim? Could a Catholic kill a Protestant if he knew of the laws of cause and effect and the journey of the soul? Could a Hindu hurt a Sikh? A Buddhist kill a Hindu? A Muslim murder a Jew?

For that matter, would an investment banker ever again look at a panhandler in the same light? Would a rage-filled husband inflict physical harm on his helpless spouse? Would a racist spit venomous vitriol at his unfortunate victim if he knew that their roles could well be reversed in the next life?

And would not wars—especially religious wars—be exposed for the laughable absurdities they actually are?

The soul of man is like to
water; from Heaven it cometh,
to Heaven it riseth…
And then returning to earth,
forever alternating.

—JOHANN WOLFGANG
VON GOETHE

Could the world, as many great scriptures claim, be one gargantuan stage upon which "soul actors" play out the great cosmic drama of Life? Could it indeed be that when the curtain descends at the close of each individual lifetime, the actors experience a period of non-judgmental evaluation and counsel, and then reemerge accoutered in different fleshly costumes to play new roles in the next act?

Is this the ageless cycle of resurrection, and ascension towards eventual union with God that all the great men and mystics mentioned earlier speak of?

Can hatred, in any form, exist in such an illusory charade played out on a fictive stage?

Every religion speaks of Love as the glue that bonds together the souls of all beings. Could there be a more effective, all-encompassing classroom than the realm of physical existence in which to learn this greatest lesson of all?

Spiritual Masters, Religious leaders,

the world's greatest Philosophers,

Visionaries, Teachers, Intellectuals,

Sages, Poets, Artists, Generals,

Scientists, Industrialists...

They all believed in reincarnation.

Are they all wrong?

*We want to lead mankind to
the place where there is neither
the Vedas, nor the Bible, nor
the Qur'an; yet this has to be
done by harmonizing the Vedas,
the Bible, and the Qur'an.*

—Swami Vivekananda

✢

CHAPTER 8

Unity

This brings us back to the salient, and more pressing, point of this discussion: how can war in the name of God ever be rationally justified by intelligent minds? How could such divisiveness, dissent, anger, brutality, and chauvinism possibly bear the message of a loving Creator?

It is desperately troubling to think that millions live and die to preserve and perpetuate this madness. The sheer scale of this insanity boggles the mind.

*The fact that astronomies change
while the stars abide is a true
analogy of every realm of human
life and thought, religion not least
of all. No existent theology can be a
final formulation of spiritual truth.*

—HARRY EMERSON FOSDICK

Would the answer, then, be to swirl the world's religions into one great ecumenical melting pot and rename them, say, "The Path"?

Would the simple, wonderfully personal, journey to communion with our Creator really require a fancier name than that? And would we need the accoutrements of war to help us on our way, when clear vision and brotherhood would get us safely there?

Isn't it time for a paradigm shift that crystallizes the underlying unity of all world religions, where the myriad names of God are universalized into something as simple as, say, "The One"? After all, is it possible to commit a faux pas by assigning Him the wrong name? Does the Creator of the infinite Cosmos have an ethnic background we might offend by doing so? Does He have a tribal identity we might

*Although he's regularly asked
to do so, God does not take
sides in American politics.*

—GEORGE J. MITCHELL

violate? Indeed, does He have a *religion* that an inappropriate name might inadvertently blaspheme?

Attempting to capture the essence of God in a name is as futile as trying to define the boundaries of infinity or the limits of eternity. God defies labeling, eludes pigeonholing, yet every religion strives to monopolize His divine grace. People even reserve His blessing for their particular country on "patriotic" bumper stickers and banners. When we encounter extraterrestrial beings—which will give rise, in our territorially-mired minds, to even newer borders—will our bumper stickers then read "God Bless Earth"?

When will we learn what the Tao Te Ching and other enlightened teachings have been expounding patiently for thousands of years,

*One person will say that his
road is by far the best, another
person will say that his road is
the best. But when both reach
their destination, they will be at
the same Goal: Truth. In Truth
there is no conflict; Truth or God-
realisation transcends all religions.*

—Sri Chinmoy

that, "good or evil, the Master doesn't take sides"?

Especially in the present age of turmoil and global upheaval, when will we acknowledge that God lavishes His impartial blessings upon *all* the countries of our planet (yes, the entire United Nations), and still has ample blessings left in His inexhaustible reservoir to spread throughout the countless other planets scattered across His Universe? When exposed to the light of logic and reason, why does this selfish vein of thinking not strike an intelligent mind as ignorant?

Because indoctrination has led us to believe that *our* religion is better than *theirs.* And we are prepared to kill to make *them* realize that *our* path to God is the only true path.

And so, as mankind continues to sing its sectarian songs, God weeps.

If religion means primarily God-consciousness, or the realization of God both within and without, and secondarily a body of beliefs, tenets, and dogmas, then, strictly speaking, there is but one religion in the world, for there is but one God.

—PARAMAHANSA YOGANANDA

✍

CHAPTER 9

The One

When people ask me about my own religion, I simply answer that I believe in God. This kind of simplicity seems to unsettle most religious people. When pushed as to whether I am a Christian, I answer yes. A Buddhist? Of course. A Hindu? Definitely. A Muslim? Undoubtedly. A Jew? Absolutely. A Catholic? Unquestionably.

The "True Believers" of the various religions find my belief in a common God troubling at best, and unpardonably blasphemous at worst.

I never told my own religion nor
scrutinized that of another. I never
attempted to make a convert, nor
wished to change another's creed.
I am satisfied that yours must
be an excellent religion to have
produced a life of such exemplary
virtue and correctness. For it is in
our lives, and not from our words,
that our religion must be judged.

—THOMAS JEFFERSON

Indeed, more than one follower of an orthodox religion has regarded me with great pity and wept over my lamentable upbringing.

Even though I consciously try not to denigrate the belief systems of others, I was once chided that my "unorthodox" philosophy was a rude attempt to strip people of their religious identities. A spurious allegation, but one that gives rise to an interesting question: What *does* constitute one's "religious identity"?

↔

Is it a bumper sticker or badge that one flaunts on a vehicle to announce to all and sundry that he is part of an exclusive "club"? Is it a special affiliation that one proudly proclaims to define his particular scriptural doctrine? Or is it reflected through unique, instantly identifiable forms of attire? Or is religious identity

*The unique personality which is
the real life in me, I can not gain
unless I search for the real life,
the spiritual quality, in others.
I am myself spiritually dead
unless I reach out to the fine
quality dormant in others. For
it is only with the god enthroned
in the innermost shrine of the
other, that the god hidden in
me, will consent to appear.*

—FELIX ADLER

linguistically implicit in the devotional names that parents assign to their offspring in some parts of the world to advertise their faith to society?

Do these extrinsic symbols of theistic affiliation define one's intrinsic religious identity? Or is true religious identity a quiet inner understanding of what all religions paraphrase as "The One In All"? Is it not the realization that each of our souls is but a spark of the eternal flame of Divine Consciousness we call God?

And is prayer not a personal, private, natural form of communication between all sentient beings in the Universe and their Maker, requiring neither intermediaries, nor brokers, nor middlemen? Is it possible that if one desires to find God, one need only look *inward* in quiet meditation and prayer?

Is not meditation the purest form of prayer?

This is my simple religion:
There is no need for temples;
no need for complicated
philosophy. Our own brain,
our own heart is our temple;
the philosophy is kindness.
—HH THE DALAI LAMA

Lighthouses are more
helpful than churches.
—BENJAMIN FRANKLIN

What is prayer, but a silent, sublime bond that connects one directly with The Source in the temple of one's own heart? Surely, prayer does not require a church, mosque, synagogue, or other similar sanctum for its fulfillment? Does it really matter *where* one chooses to pray?

Which brings to mind the story of the black man in the old South who was denied entry to an all-white church. Miserable after years of trying in vain he went home to his hovel and prayed to God with great intensity. God appeared to him and said, "Don't feel sad, my son. You are not alone in your quest. I, too, have been trying to get into that church since it was built, but to no avail."

Our Creator speaks to every one of us, not in the concrete temples of our own creation, but in the silent temples of our souls—the "kingdom of heaven" within. And His true

*It is impossible to find God
outside of ourselves. Our own
souls contribute all of the divinity
that is outside of us. We are the
greatest temple. The objectification
is only a faint imitation of what
we see within ourselves.*

—SWAMI VIVEKANANDA

word does not appear on the sectarian scrolls written by men, whose sad misinterpretations perpetuate our petty earthly divisions and conflicts.

God's true word is inscribed on a faceless slate, in a wordless script, in the formless realm of the soul that lies within all sentient beings.

The beginning of love is to
let those we love be perfectly
themselves, and not to twist them
to fit our own image. Otherwise
we love only the reflection of
ourselves we find in them.

—THOMAS MERTON

⇔

CHAPTER 10

Children

When the religious dust begins to settle on our planet, we can turn to an ancient sacred text, which lovingly reassures us, "As unnecessary as a well is to a village on the banks of a river, so unnecessary are all scriptures to someone who has seen the Truth. When your understanding has passed beyond the thicket of delusions, there is nothing you need to learn from even the most sacred scripture."

When we can sense that something so fundamental is so intuitively correct, how is it

In religion…people's beliefs and convictions are in almost every case gotten at second-hand, and without examination, from authorities who have not themselves examined the questions at issue but have taken them at second-hand from other non-examiners, whose opinions about them were not worth a brass farthing.

—MARK TWAIN

that, century upon century, millennium upon millennium, our earthly religions sustain and perpetuate their divisive dogmatic messages?

They do this by ensuring that we accept their teachings without question, as we have discussed. But there's more: we are also expected to force these beliefs down the innocent throats of our offspring.

This is the most unconscionable sacrilege.

Children's minds see worlds of beauty that we adults, blinded by our beliefs, cannot touch or comprehend. We owe it to them to let their unique, precious souls blossom on their own, unbridled by *our* concepts, *our* superstitions, *our* insecurities, *our* prejudices (which we inherited from *our* parents, and they, from theirs).

From infancy, we painstakingly build doctrinal boxes around our children, and yet, once

God creates each soul differently,
so that when all the mud
is finally cleared away,
His light will shine through
it in a beautiful, colorful,
totally new pattern.

—M. SCOTT PECK

they reach adulthood, we urge them to "think outside" the very boxes in which we have imprisoned them. Later on, they will build the same boxes around *their* children.

But this cycle of insanity *can* be broken.

In the words of a great, saintly poet, "Our children come through us, but they are not of us... you may strive to be like them, but seek not to make them like you."

We like to think they are of us and "belong" to us, but in reality our parental functions are that of conduits... mere portals that open these newborns' lives unto them.

Our children are God's unique creations, imbued with their own exquisite souls, and on their own individual journeys. They, too, are visitors to this transient material plane, equipped to enact their own dramas and direct their own destinies—but alas, they are often

*Don't limit a child to your
own learning, for he was
born in another time.*

—RABBINICAL SAYING

handicapped by the conditioning we parents force upon them.

The great spiritual master of a major religion once said about children, "Do not hinder them, for to such belongs the kingdom of God." Another time, as his disciples were arguing about who was the greatest, he brought a child before them and said, "Unless you turn and become like children, you will never enter the kingdom of heaven."

Turn and become like children? How *can* we, when we spend our lives trying to make them like *us*? With all our good intentions to save them, we unwittingly enslave them.

↭

I am perfectly at peace with the fact that my teenage son is being reared as a true, God-loving (as opposed to God-*fearing*) citizen of

Love expects no reward.

Love knows no fear.

Love Divine

Gives—does not demand.

Love thinks no evil;

imputes no motive.

To Love is to share and serve.

—Sivananda

the Universe. He is made aware of the teachings of all religions—both the common-sense goodness that permeates them and the allegorical curiosities that dilute them.

His language of thought is rooted in intuition and reason, not doctrine and fear.

He is gently guided—never coerced—to question all socially transmitted notions and beliefs that run counter to common sense.

He is taught that the language of the Creator is intuition, imagination, inspiration, creativity, intent, understanding, and, above all, unconditional love.

In the final analysis, is this not the true religious experience?

I thank God for granting me the wisdom *not* to stamp my child with some medieval branding iron, or plaster him with some meaningless

*All children are artists. The
problem is how to remain an
artist once he grows up.*
—PABLO PICASSO

*When I approach a child, he
inspires in me two sentiments:
tenderness for what he is, and
respect for what he may become.*
—LOUIS PASTEUR

label, or bind him with fear to some mindless practice.

I hope that he will grow up with an attitude of unfettered curiosity, compassion, and love. He will be free to think, and act, as *he* chooses. His spirituality will evolve from his own un-tarnished God-given canvas, upon which he is free to paint.

His creed is Love; his religion, the Path; his destination, the One.

When my son is grown, of course, he will be perfectly free to choose whatever path pleases him—but I doubt that a free mind would strive to be caged.

*Religion is a set of social
and political institutions and
spirituality is a private pursuit
which may or may not take
place in a church setting.*
—D. PATRICK MILLER

⌀

CHAPTER 11

Freedom

I believe that future generations of souls, thus emancipated by their parents, will finally help bring sanity to this world, end these wars waged in the name of God, raise the consciousness of Man, and help make this planet a better place.

Only an appreciation of the following truth shall ultimately set man free:

Religions divide. Spirituality unites.

*How much easier your task and
mine might be…if suddenly there
was a threat to this world from
another species from another planet
outside in the Universe. We'd forget
all the little local differences that
we have between our countries,
and we would find out once and for
all that we really are all human
beings here on this earth together.*

—PRESIDENT RONALD REAGAN, TO
SOVIET LEADER MIKHAIL GORBACHEV
DURING THE GENEVA SUMMIT
CONFERENCE IN NOVEMBER 1985

Albert Einstein presciently expressed this same truth when he said, "The religion of the future will be a Cosmic religion."

I humbly offer that this great man's prophetic words encapsulate everything I have striven to express in this book.

Indeed, I have labored to ensure that all the sayings quoted in this book—many of which I have borrowed from some of the most illumined minds that ever lived—support that basic message. I believe that they collectively constitute Essential Thinking For The New Millennium. And for this, I owe every one of their authors, alive or not, my deepest gratitude. Through their words, they have gifted us with their wisdom and knowledge, but the rest is up to us.

Until we find within ourselves the courage and confidence to break out of the doctrinal

*True religion is...living with
all one's soul, with all one's
goodness and righteousness.*

—ALBERT EINSTEIN

cages that have kept us apart since time imme-morial, we humans are doomed to continue our mad fratricidal butchery—and, quite possibly, face extinction at our own hands.

Spiritual awakening, on a global scale, can only ensue from Cosmic thinking.

For us to think in Cosmic terms, we need to shake ourselves out of this hereditary Earth-centered trance, climb out of our primordial "well," gaze up at the heavens, and open our minds to the awesome Reality of which our planet is but an infinitesimal speck.

We must learn to move beyond our ingrained, Narcissistic self-image as "the chosen ones" of all Creation, and, humbling though it will be, begin to think of ourselves as cohabitants of a boundless Universe bristling with life.

Regardless of what the rest of the "count-less billion life-forms" may be, or what strange

We carry within us the
wonders we seek without us.

—SIR THOMAS BROWNE

"worlds" they may inhabit, we must learn to appreciate that the Force that permeates *all* life emanates from The One Creative Source.

Only such a substantive shift in our thinking will enable us to begin the task of tearing down the sectarian walls that have divided this planet for millennia. Only then will we see our illusory cages for what they are, and realize the utter insanity of the wars we wage in the name of God.

If we are to survive as a species in this new millennium, it is vital that we awaken to this new way of thinking.

The time is *now*.

⟁

God has no religion.

—MAHATHMA GANDHI

Thank you Mom,
For having opened my mind
with that 4,000-year-old
soul-stirring prayer
to the One...

Oh Supreme Divine...
Thou art the Creator of the Universe
Of all worlds, space, and Heaven;
We adore Thy radiant splendor,
Thy Pure Form;
Oh Source of all Creation,
We humbly meditate upon
Thy divine radiance;
Thee we behold,
Inspire all our thoughts,
Guide our soul,
Open our mind's eye,
The eye of Wisdom.

About the Author

Nila Sagadevan was born in Ceylon (now Sri Lanka) and educated in Britain. Born in a predominantly Buddhist country to liberal-minded Hindu parents who encouraged belief in a single Creator, he was sent at the age of 5 to Christian boarding schools where he read the Bible, attended Sunday school, and sang in the school choir.

An aeronautical engineer-turned-pilot, Sagadevan left Scotland for America in 1972. He lived in Alaska for 15 years when a profound, life-altering experience changed his concept of earthly religions forever, and caused him to deeply ponder the anthropocentric mindset that guides human life. His quest for knowledge and self-inquiry has led him on a journey through more than 40 countries and to many of the centers of the world's major religions.

Sagadevan, who was the featured guest in a television documentary on extraterrestrial phenomena, also produced his own radio show, *The Open Mind,* in the 1980s. The program, which discussed declassified government documents obtained through the *Freedom Of Information Act,* reached millions of listeners in the US and Europe. His writings, on a variety of subjects, have appeared in numerous publications. He lives in Southern California, and may be reached at: nila@truepennymedia.com

Available at your local bookstore.

To order additional copies online, please visit:
www.WarpaintOfTheGods.com

Audio CDs (narrated by the author) are also available.

To order by mail:
Books: USD 12.00 / CAD 14.50 / EUR 9.50 / AUD 15.50
CDs: USD 14:00 / CAD 17.50 / EUR 11.00 / AUD 18.00
For information on volume discounts, please contact:
support@TruepennyMedia.com

Please add appropriate S&H charges (see below),
make check payable (in US Dollars) and mail to:

Truepenny Media, Inc.
PO Box 2177
Laguna Hills, CA
USA 92654-2177

Shipping and Handling Charges:
(US Postal Service, First Class Mail)

Books:
    USA - $3.75 (Each additional book, add $2.75)
    CAN - $4.00 ($3.00)
    EUR - $7.50 ($6.50)
    AUD - $8.50 ($7.50)

Audio CDs:
    USA - $3.25 (Each additional CD, add $2.00)
    CAN - $3.50 ($2.50)
    EUR - $5.25 ($4.25)
    AUD - $5.50 ($4.50)